15-minute
COUNSELING
TECHNIQUES
THAT WORK

WHAT YOU DIDN'T
LEARN IN GRAD SCHOOL

NATIONAL CENTER for
YOUTH ISSUES

15-Minute Counseling Techniques that Work
What You Didn't Learn in Grad School

By Allison Edwards

"The counselor is not the strategy. The counselor teaches strategies."

As counselors, we spend our days helping kids. Kids come to us with a variety of problems, searching for answers outside of themselves. They want us to fix situations, listen to their problems, or give them solutions for the issues they are facing. While these strategies may work temporarily, we really never help kids until we give them tools—or techniques—to manage thoughts and feelings on their own. Our job is not to do it for them. Our job is to teach them how to do it themselves. This is the greatest gift we can give.

HOW TO USE THIS MANUAL:

Each of the techniques in this manual can be used individually or in a group with children ages K–12. In some techniques, I suggest using materials such as clay, yarn, or beads with younger children, but you may be surprised how many older children like to use them as well! You can modify the techniques based on the developmental level of the child and make adjustments depending on the needs of your specific population.

I would recommend teaching only one technique during each counseling session. Then, write each technique on a blank 5x8 index card to send home with the child. This reinforces the technique and helps parents stay involved in what you are doing during sessions.

OTHER IMPORTANT THINGS TO KNOW:

1. **The Relationship is Most Important:** This book is about techniques, but the greatest techniques will not work if you don't first connect with a child. Connection happens in the first few moments of the session when you look at a child and ask, "How are you?" For many kids, this will be the only time they are ever asked that question. From there, you will want to acknowledge where the child is at that moment and create a safe space by showing a child, "I hear you. I believe you. I understand you. I accept you. I respect you." From there, you can begin teaching techniques.

2. **Talk in Numbers:** Techniques will only work if a child is calm enough to use them. In working with any child, develop a number scale to gauge the child's feelings—with 1 being the least intense and 10 being the most intense. A 10 will look very different to each child. Some kids yell at a 10, and other kids shut down and won't talk at all. Help a child determine what their 10 is, what their 5 is, and so on, so you (and they) will know what tools will be effective at which times. Techniques will only be helpful when a child is at an 8 or below. After a child reaches an 8 or above, the child is considered "flooded" and is unable to think clearly or use a technique effectively. When a child is "flooded," they need to reset the brain by changing the five senses. You can help a child identify what spaces inside the school will help them reset. Some kids may benefit from carrying a bandana with drops of lavender oil to smell during the day. Other kids may want to run cool water on their hands in the bathroom. It's important to teach kids when they should use techniques and when they need to reset. It is important to teach parents, administrators, and teachers this as well.

3. **Follow-up:** One of our most important jobs is to help kids become accountable. We can teach effective tools, but if we don't remind children to use them, we won't

prepare them for being able to manage emotions on their own. You can reinforce techniques by following up with the child at the beginning of the next session. Ask the child how the technique is working, how it has been useful, and how often they've used it. The follow-up is important because it makes the child an active participant, promotes buy-in, and helps the child take ownership of managing their feelings.

Now, let's get started!

TECHNIQUE ONE

SQUARE BREATHING

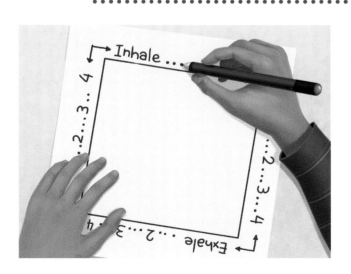

15-Minute Counseling Techniques that Work *What You Didn't Learn in Grad School*

SQUARE BREATHING

MATERIALS NEEDED

5x8 blank index card

WHO CAN BENEFIT

Any child needing to calm the mind and body

WHY IT WORKS

This technique engages both the mind (by counting) and the body (by breathing). When you ask a child to breathe without counting, they will remain focused on the problem. This tool takes the focus off of the problem and allows both the mind and body to relax.

HOW TO IMPLEMENT:

1. On a 5x8 blank index card, draw a square (similar to this example), with Inhale . . . 2 . . . 3 . . . 4 on the top side, Hold . . . 2 . . . 3 . . . 4 on the right side, Exhale . . . 2 . . . 3 . . . 4 on the bottom side, and Rest . . . 2 . . . 3 . . . 4 on the left side.

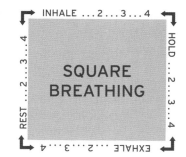

2. Hold up the 5x8 card and ask the child, "How many sides are there in a square?" When the child answers "four," say, "That's right. Today I am going to show you a technique called Square Breathing. We call it Square Breathing because everything we do is going to be to the count of 4."

3. Explain the activity: "In this activity we are going to relax our minds and our bodies. We're going to take in deep breaths and count on our fingers at the same time." Ask the child to lift up their fingers and count, 1, 2, 3, 4. Then say, "Now let's practice together."

4. Inhale: "Let's start by breathing in for four seconds. Let's pretend you walk into your house and smell chocolate chip cookies baking in the oven. You are going to breathe in that amazing smell for four seconds while counting on your fingers. Ready? Inhale . . . 2 . . . 3 . . . 4."

5. Hold: "Next, let's hold the smell of cookies in our nose. Stay completely relaxed and still. We're going to hold our breath for 4 seconds. Ready? Hold . . . 2 . . . 3 . . . 4." It's important that children do not puff their cheeks out or hold any tension in their body during this step. If they do, redirect them back to a relaxed face that is holding the sweet smell of chocolate chip cookies in their nose.

6. Exhale: "Now, let's slowly breathe out like we are blowing on the chocolate chip cookies to cool them. Let's count to four, using our fingers. Ready? Exhale . . . 2 . . . 3 . . . 4."

7. Rest: "Now, let's rest for four seconds, letting our bodies relax. You can count on your fingers. Ready? Rest . . . 2 . . . 3 . . . 4."

8. Repeat this four-step sequence three times in a row with the child until you feel they have mastered all four steps.

9. Wrap up the activity by saying, "This activity will help us go from feeling like uncooked spaghetti (hold your body very straight and rigid, modeling how this would look) to feeling like cooked spaghetti (move your arms and body

around loosely). If you've ever held uncooked spaghetti, you know it will break or snap under any amount of pressure, but cooked spaghetti is flexible and able to handle a lot of pressure. Use Square Breathing when you are feeling a lot of pressure, and you can become like cooked spaghetti!"

10. Create follow-through at home by giving the child the index card and saying, "Now I want you to go home and teach your parents how to do Square Breathing. I also would like you to practice three times in a row each night before bed. This will help you sleep better and learn Square Breathing well enough to use it anytime you need."

15-Minute Counseling Techniques that Work   *What You Didn't Learn in Grad School*

TECHNIQUE TWO

CHANGE THE CHANNEL

2 CHANGE THE CHANNEL

MATERIALS NEEDED

clay in various colors, scissors, 5x8 blank index card

WHO CAN BENEFIT

Kids who are stuck on a thought, can't let go of negative thinking, or are worried, sad, or overwhelmed

WHY IT WORKS

Kids are concrete thinkers and thoughts are abstract. In order for kids to understand how to change thoughts, they must have a concrete way to understand them. Change the Channel allows kids to replace negative thoughts with positive ones in a way they can developmentally understand.

HOW TO IMPLEMENT:

1. Flatten out a ball of clay about the size of a tennis ball into the shape of a remote control. Then flatten out another small piece of clay (about the size of a golf ball) and cut out small shapes with scissors to make buttons that the child will later place on the remote control. (I prefer to do this part prior to the session as it saves time and helps the child focus on the strategy rather than how to make the remote control.)

2. Say to the child, "Your brain is like a television with a bunch of different channels—or thoughts. Some of the channels are positive and some of them are negative. Sometimes our televisions can get stuck on a negative channel, but the good news is that you have the remote control. You can choose what you think about! Today, we are going to do an activity to help you replace negative thoughts with positive ones. We are going to use your remote control to Change the Channel."

3. Ask, "What negative thought(s) are you having that you want to replace?" The child may automatically know what the thought is (e.g. "I am going fail") or need help identifying the thought. After you've identified the thought, say, "Now, number how intense that thought is from 1 to 10." (Use the number scale explained in the introduction.) For example, a child might say, "I feel I'm going to fail at a 9."

4. Next, say, "Now I want you to choose a replacement thought. Think of something that makes you feel happy or excited at the same level of intensity as the negative thought you just had." This is very important because choosing a thought that is not as intense (such as "I am going to succeed") will not be strong enough to change the negative thought. Good examples of replacement thoughts are things kids are looking forward to such as birthdays, holidays, or time off school.

5. Say, "Now, take a look at the clay in front of you. We are going to build a remote control by adding buttons that can change the channels. But first, let's remember your negative thoughts and go through them one by one, replacing them with positive thoughts." Have kids mention a negative thought and a positive replacement thought. "Now, you can put a button on your remote, and whenever you have that negative thought, you can simply push the button and change the channel!" Allow kids to go through several negative thoughts and replacement thoughts, adding buttons to their remote as they go. Then, ask the student to practice Changing the

Channel while they're in your office by having them close their eyes and bring the negative thought to mind ("I am going to fail"). Once the child is focused on the thought, say "click" and have the child immediately change the thought. It looks like this:

6. Write the above on a blank index card and have the child take it home (along with the remote control). A clay remote control should dry within twenty-four hours, and then the child can put the remote in their backpack or in their desk as a reminder of how to Change the Channel.

15-Minute Counseling Techniques that Work *What You Didn't Learn in Grad School*

TECHNIQUE THREE

ALL
TANGLED UP

··

3 ALL TANGLED UP

MATERIALS NEEDED

yarn, scissors

WHO CAN BENEFIT

Kids who are overwhelmed, take too much on, are overachievers, or have a hard time managing stress

WHY IT WORKS

This technique gives kids a visual representation of what's going on in their minds. By seeing all the ways they are tangled up mentally, they are able to make choices about what they are willing to let go of.

HOW TO IMPLEMENT:

1. Holding a ball of yarn, tell the child that you are going to do an activity to help untangle their mind. Say, "We're going to make a brain tangle so we can get a better idea of what's going on in your mind." Start the activity by tying the yarn in a knot around a chair or table leg on one side of the office.

2. Next, say, "Now, I want you to take this ball of yarn, loop it around something on the other side of the room, and

tell me what has you tangled up." The child will take the ball of yarn, loop it around something, and say, "I get tangled up when _____." (You may need to demonstrate this for the child.)

3. The child will continue with the next thing that gets them tangled up, looping the yarn around another object. They will continue this process until they have named all of the things that have them tangled up.

4. Once the child has finished the tangled web, sit for a few minutes and process what they created. Ask them, "How does it feel to see all these tangles in your mind?" You can also provide feedback by saying, "There are a lot of tangles here. You must feel overwhelmed."

5. Hand the child a pair of scissors and say, "Sometimes when we have too much going on and so many things tangled up in our brains, we need to let go of some things. What are you willing to let go of?" The child will then cut the tangles one by one, calling out what they are willing to let go of. As the child cuts the strands of yarn, the tension will release in the web and you can see it lose its strength. It's okay if children want to hold on to some of the tangles. They may not be ready to let go, and that is fine. What's important is they have ownership of the things they want to keep and what they want to let go of.

6. After the child is finished with the activity, give them the tangles as a reminder of how busy and tangled up the brain can get. You can also give the child a ball of yarn to use at home. This will allow kids to use the tool on their own.

TECHNIQUE FOUR

WORRY JAR

WORRY JAR

MATERIALS NEEDED

clay, strips of paper (or beads)

WHO CAN BENEFIT

Kids who worry or have a lot of stress or concerns

WHY IT WORKS

Children are concrete thinkers and feelings are abstract. Making a worry jar gives kids a concrete place to put their worries so they don't have to keep them in their mind.

HOW TO IMPLEMENT:

1. Cut strips of paper and make a clay pinch pot prior to session. This will save time and potential stress on the child who may focus more on making the pinch pot than on the purpose of the exercise. How to make a pinch pot: roll a small piece of clay into a ball. Push your thumbs into the middle of the ball until you almost reach the bottom. Pinch around the sides of the jar to make the jar expand. When the jar gets approximately one inch thick, you can stop pinching. If you pinch too much, the jar will become flimsy and break.

2. At the beginning of the session, ask the child to write down one worry on each strip of paper. If the child is too young to write, use beads to represent their worries. If the child doesn't like to write or if they struggle with spelling, write for them.

3. Hold up the worry jar and say, "This is a worry jar. The worries you just talked about can either stay in your head or we can put them in this jar, but they cannot be in both places." Children will understand this as they are concrete thinkers.

4. Then, ask the child to put each worry into the jar while saying, "Worry Jar, please hold this for me." This allows the child to let go of the worry.

5. Encourage the child to tear up the worry strips once a specific worry ends (For example, if the child was worried about a math test, they would rip up the worry once the test is over). This teaches kids that worries come and go, and it helps them feel excited once they accomplish something hard.

6. Allow the child to take their worry jar home with them. Explain that the worry jar can be used at any time. If they are unable to talk with you or another safe person, they can simply write their worries down and have the worry jar hold them until they have an opportunity to talk about them. If they don't want to talk about them, that's fine too.

TECHNIQUE FIVE

BRAIN PLATE

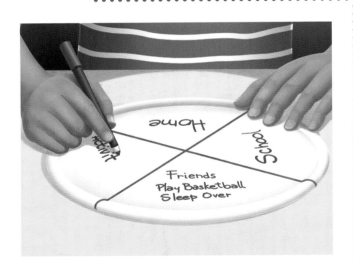

15-Minute Counseling Techniques that Work   *What You Didn't Learn in Grad School*

5 BRAIN PLATE

MATERIALS NEEDED

paper plate, marker, pencil

WHO CAN BENEFIT

Kids who are overwhelmed, take too much on, or put too much pressure on themselves

WHY IT WORKS

This technique simplifies how to manage stress by teaching kids how to focus on today only. It helps kids see that today's problems are manageable, but when you overload your brain, stress ensues. It simplifies how to choose what to focus on by giving kids specific instructions on how to decide.

HOW TO IMPLEMENT:

1. Tell the child, "Your brain is like a dinner plate. If you overload it and eat too much, you won't feel very well. If I asked you to eat a week's worth of food in one sitting you would get sick, right?" Allow the child to respond. "That's what you're doing to your brain if you take on too much. You're overloading your brain and that's why you feel overwhelmed."

2. With the marker, draw four equal sections on a paper plate and write the words "Home," "School," "Friends," and "Activities" in each section (like the example above, one word per section). Explain that these four areas represent the different parts of our lives and the responsibilities we have in each. And each responsibility we have takes up thoughts and space in our brain.

3. Ask the child, "What's on your brain plate today?"

4. Have the child write in pencil what is on their plate for that day only. Help the child think about what they need to focus on today.

5. Turn the plate over and, in marker, write: "If it's not on your plate, get rid of it." Explain to the child that when their mind feels overloaded with new thoughts and responsibilities, they can ask the question: "Are you on my plate for today?" If the answer is no, they can remove that thought from their brain plate.

6. Allow the child to take the paper plate home with them and encourage them to do this on their own. Tell them they can erase the words on their plate each evening and begin each morning by writing (in pencil) what is on their plate for that day.

TECHNIQUE SIX

MY TOP 5

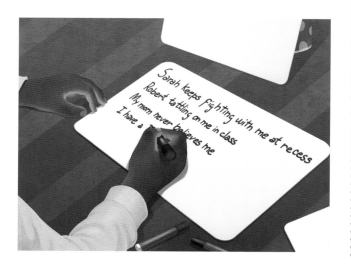

15-Minute Counseling Techniques that Work *What You Didn't Learn in Grad School*

MY TOP 5

MATERIALS NEEDED

whiteboard, whiteboard marker

WHO CAN BENEFIT

Kids who are overwhelmed with worries or problems, have a hard time focusing on one issue, and have a hard time staying on topic in sessions

WHY IT WORKS

This technique gives kids a boundary so they can sort out what is really important to them. It helps them see a visual of what they are overwhelmed by, what they can let go of, and what they need to focus on.

HOW TO IMPLEMENT:

1. Hand the child a whiteboard and ask them to write down everything they're worried about or see as a problem. Allow them to take as much time as they need to complete this. (This can be frustrating for kids who want to talk about all of their problems, but it is helpful for them to pause and take the time to write them down.)

2. Ask the child to erase all but five problems from the board. This can be difficult for kids who want to hold on

to things and try to solve them, but, even so, encourage them to erase all but five.

3. Have the child rank the problems one to five, with one being the biggest problem and five being the smallest. Once the child has determined this, you can begin talking about problem number one and then work your way down the list. How you approach each problem is not as important as having the child prioritize what's most important to them. For some problems, you may have them use a coping technique (such as Square Breathing), and for others you may need to just listen. The process of narrowing problems down to five might take most of your session, but it helps kids slow down long enough to really look at what is going on in their minds.

4. Encourage kids to do this on their own. If they're overwhelmed at home or school, they can use this tool to help identify their problems, prioritize them, and know what to focus on—all on their own. They can also do this prior to meeting with you so they can start the session with their main concerns, thus having a more productive session.

TECHNIQUE SEVEN

SICK OF EGGS

SICK OF EGGS

MATERIALS NEEDED

plastic eggs, strips of paper

WHO CAN BENEFIT

Kids who struggle with emotion regulation, are angry or frustrated, or have a hard time verbalizing feelings

WHY IT WORKS

This technique allows kids to let out frustrations in a safe way. By giving kids an outlet and normalizing the expression of negative emotions, kids can leave your office feeling much more relaxed and regulated.

HOW TO IMPLEMENT:

1. Introduce the technique by asking kids to share what they're sick of. This approach encompasses all feelings, including sadness, worry, frustration, anger, and so on, and it allows kids to share what they're struggling with.

2. Say, "I'd like you to write each of the things you're sick of on a strip of paper" (one strip for each thing). Give the child time to do this. If they have difficulty writing or spelling, you can write them down for them. It's more

important to reduce stress during the activity than to require them to write.

3. Show them the plastic eggs and explain that a strip of paper will go inside each egg. Direct the child to a clear wall and ask them to, one at a time, place a strip of paper inside an egg and throw the egg at the wall in front of them while saying, "I'm sick of [whatever is written on the paper inside the egg]!"

4. Steer clear of the wall, as eggs can come flying off the wall pretty fast. Watch the eggs break apart as they hit the wall. In doing this, you will help normalize that we all get sick of things and letting out frustration is very important.

5. This tool is unique in that I do not send eggs home with kids as they can use them to let out frustrations in not-so-therapeutic ways (i.e. hitting other kids with them).

TECHNIQUE EIGHT

GIVE YOUR FEELING A NAME

8 GIVE YOUR FEELING A NAME

MATERIALS NEEDED

clay, markers

WHO CAN BENEFIT

Kids who struggle with self-esteem, feel they will never get better, label themselves with a mental health diagnosis (anxiety, depression, etc.), or are debilitated by their feelings

WHY IT WORKS

This technique empowers kids to see that they are not controlled by their feelings. Feelings come and go, and if you befriend them instead of trying to make them go away, you gain control. It is also a fun activity that takes the power out of negative emotions.

HOW TO IMPLEMENT:

1. Ask the child, "What does your feeling (worry, anger, sadness, etc.) look like?" If a child struggles to identify this, you can ask additional questions like: "What color is it? Does it have big eyes? Does it have teeth? How big is it?" You can also make your own feeling out of clay (I highly recommend this!) to help normalize that we all

have feelings and struggle with how to manage them. Once you create your own feeling, I would encourage you to keep it on your desk. Then, whenever you begin this activity in the future, you can introduce your feeling to children.

2. Give the child a ball of clay and allow them to make their feeling. Talk with them as they're creating it and comment on the features they've created (e.g. Your feeling has big eyes, large teeth, or is very scary looking).

3. Help the child name their feeling. This may take a few minutes to come up with, but the child can choose any name that fits. (It may help to share the name you've given your feeling.) Some examples are Worry Walter or Spazzy Sam. Other kids might choose a simple name like Frank. This is a very fun way to take the power out of the feeling. And they can begin referring to their feeling by its name.

4. Say, "Now that your feeling has a name, instead of saying, 'I was really worried today,' you can say, 'Worry Wanda showed up during math class, but she left when I went to lunch.'" This will encourage kids to see that they aren't always debilitated by feelings but that feelings come and go.

5. Allow the child to take their feeling home with them and encourage them to let it dry in a safe place (like on their nightstand) for twenty-four hours.

6. During the follow-up session, ask the child how Wanda or Walter or Frank is doing. Begin using this new language so kids can see their feelings as temporary and realize that they don't have to be debilitated by them.

TECHNIQUE NINE

GRIEF LEAF

15-Minute Counseling Techniques that Work   *What You Didn't Learn in Grad School*

GRIEF LEAF

MATERIALS NEEDED

leaf, markers

WHO CAN BENEFIT

Kids who are struggling with feelings of grief or loss, have a hard time putting their feelings into words, need a concrete way to understand abstract emotions

WHY IT WORKS

This technique helps kids understand and process their feelings before and after a loss by getting their feelings out of their head and onto an object. It helps kids have a visual representation of what they're feeling. Kids enjoy finding the right leaf for them, and it helps them have ownership of their experience.

HOW TO IMPLEMENT:

1. Take a walk outside and ask the child to find a leaf. It doesn't need to be a specific kind of leaf, just one they like or are drawn to.

2. Return to the counseling office (or if it's a nice day, stay outside) and tell the child that this activity they are about

to do will help them identify the feelings they've had before and after their loss.

3. On one side of the leaf, ask the child to write down feelings they had before the loss. If the leaf has five points, they can write down a feeling word on each point, or simply write the words randomly on the leaf. Some kids might want to draw a picture of the feeling, and that is fine too.

4. When they are finished, ask the child to flip the leaf over and write down the feelings they've had after the loss. These could be feelings they are currently having or had directly after the loss. What you want the child to process is how grief creates a variety of feelings you might not have had before. It's also important to explain that grief is like a roller coaster. Feelings come and go very quickly. Sometimes you feel okay or even good and other times you can feel really low or sad.

5. Allow the child to take their leaf home with them if they'd like. Counselors could even make several leaves and press them against waxed paper to hang in a window. This will help normalize the feelings of grief and loss with children who do this activity.

"I DID IT!" LIST

15-Minute Counseling Techniques that Work   *What You Didn't Learn in Grad School*

TECHNIQUE TEN

10 "I DID IT!" LIST

MATERIALS NEEDED

paper, pen, or pencil

WHO CAN BENEFIT

Children struggling with self-esteem, low confidence, anxiety, or depression

WHY IT WORKS

Kids can see their accomplishments written in their own handwriting and gain confidence to do other hard things. This technique overrides negative thinking by showing concrete examples of what kids have accomplished. Instead of trying to convince them they are capable of doing something hard, they can see it for themselves. Kids can keep these for years and keep adding hard things they've accomplished to the list.

HOW TO IMPLEMENT:

1. Using a piece of paper (notebook paper, printer paper, or construction paper all work fine), write "I Did It!" at the top of the page. Then, create three columns on the page and write the following words at the top of each column: Date, Activity, and Signature:

"I Did It!"

DATE	ACTIVITY	SIGNATURE
_____	_____	_____
_____	_____	_____
_____	_____	_____

2. Ask the child to write down any recent accomplishments they have had. Then, they can fill in the date and sign their name next to that activity.

3. If they want to set a goal, they can write down something they are hoping to do in the activity column. Then, whenever they have accomplished the Goal, they can fill in the Date and Signature.

4. Send the list home with the child and encourage them to continue doing hard things by saying, "I hope you will keep adding to your 'I Did It!' list." You can communicate with parents to encourage their child as well. This support will help kids take ownership of their goals. It will also encourage them to use self-motivation to accomplish what they hope to do.

5. When you meet with a child following the activity, ask what they have recently added to their list. Keep encouraging them by helping them brainstorm activities they can add and praise them for the things they have already accomplished.

TECHNIQUE ELEVEN

STRUCTURE THE UNSTRUCTURED

12 FEELINGS TRACKER

MATERIALS NEEDED

calendar, pen, 5x8 index card

WHO CAN BENEFIT

Kids who come into your office in crisis, kids who always seem to be at a ten, have trouble self-regulating, and/or have difficulty recalling past emotions

WHY IT WORKS

This technique helps both the child and the counselor gain perspective on how the child feels throughout the day. By writing down the intensity of feelings (from one to ten) during a given day, the child can learn to identify triggers and patterns which will shed light into a child's emotional world.

HOW TO IMPLEMENT:

1. Develop a number scale (refer back to the introduction for instructions) with the child based on the specific feeling you are helping them with (sadness, worry, anger, etc.). Ask the child what a ten would look like for them (trouble breathing, panic, can't think, etc.), then identify what a five might look like (anxious thoughts,

a little distracted, etc.) and so on. Every child will have a different looking number scale based on how emotions are experienced.

2. Ask the child to begin tracking the intensity of their feeling throughout the day. They can do this in a simple notebook or on a blank sheet of paper. The child may write down an eight during math class and a two during social studies. This information will help both the counselor and child identify what is triggering the feeling.

3. Write down possible triggers that are causing a spike in the child's feeling. For example, if the child has a low grade in math or has trouble getting along with the teacher, this might explain why the number is so high in math class. There may also be another student who is triggering a high emotion. The purpose of this step is to help the child identify triggering situations and determine if they can be changed or not. The purpose of this step is not to remove triggers (e.g. get students in a different class) but to help children learn how they respond to specific triggers in a healthy way.

4. Help the student identify coping strategies that will help when their emotions get high. You can refer to the other techniques in this book (Square Breathing, Change the Channel, etc.) for coping tools. It's important to have buy-in from the child in choosing the tool that will work for them. You can write down tools on strips of paper or on a 5x8 index card.

TECHNIQUE THIRTEEN

BREAKING
IT DOWN

13 BREAKING IT DOWN

MATERIALS NEEDED

dominos

WHO CAN BENEFIT

Kids who are extreme in thinking, see events as all good or all bad, complain of having the "worst day ever," and/or make blanket statements (worst, never, always)

WHY IT WORKS

This technique helps the child move out of extreme thinking to see that both good and bad things happen most every day. The dominos are a concrete way to help children deal with abstract feelings.

HOW TO IMPLEMENT:

1. When a child comes to you with an extreme reaction to something, ask them to tell you what happened in order of events. This slows the brain down and helps the child really think about what occurred. For example, if the child says, "I'm having the worst day ever," you would ask, "What was the first thing that happened this morning?" They might respond, "My mom yelled at

me when I woke up." At that point, you would place a domino on the table in front of the child and ask, "What happened next?"

2. As the child goes through the events of the day, continue to place the dominos in a row in front of the child. There should be no judgment in any of the statements the child makes, only acceptance of what the child is saying. You want to line up one domino for each thing the child reports. If a child only reports the bad things, ask more questions like, "Did you walk with anyone to class?" or "Who did you sit by at lunch?" This helps the child see the events in the middle, not just the triggering events.

3. Once the child is finished telling you about their day, ask them to look at all of the dominos. Explain that some of the dominos represent good things and some represent bad things. Ask the child to remove the dominos that represent the bad things that happened ("My mom yelled at me when I woke up" or "I forgot my science homework") and see how the day looks without them.

4. Then, replace the dominos in the line and ask the child to remove a domino for each of the good things that happened and leave only the dominos representing the bad things. Explain how when you remove any of the dominos, you leave holes in your day. Help them understand that it takes both the good and the bad to make a complete day.

5. You can also use this activity to help children realize "the domino effect" in their behavior. If they got in trouble, you can help them recall the events leading up to the incident by using one domino to explain each action. For example, if the child says, "I walked into class and someone laughed at me," you would set a domino down and ask, "What happened next?" When the child tells you the next thing that happened, you'd lay down another domino, and so on. Once the child has recalled every action that happened, ask, "What could you have done differently?" You can remove a domino representing the action they could have changed. Then

show what happens when you remove one or more dominos from the line. The whole row won't fall down because every domino plays a part in the outcome of the incident. When a child chooses something different, the whole outcome will change.

15-Minute Counseling Techniques that Work   *What You Didn't Learn in Grad School*

TECHNIQUE FOURTEEN

"WHAT I'M GOOD AT" JAR

15-Minute Counseling Techniques that Work   *What You Didn't Learn in Grad School*

14 "WHAT I'M GOOD AT" JAR

MATERIALS NEEDED

clay, beads (or strips of paper)

WHO CAN BENEFIT

Kids with low self-esteem or low confidence, kids who are experiencing a loss

WHY IT WORKS

This tool is a tangible way for kids to see what they're good at. Asking children what they like about themselves is often too difficult for them to answer. Asking them what they're good at is easier for them to identify.

HOW TO IMPLEMENT:

1. Make a pinch pot or jar out of clay (Refer to Technique 4: Worry Jar for instructions on making a pinch pot. It should be sturdy enough to hold the beads or strips of paper). You can either make the jar yourself or have the child make it. However, the focus should not be on making the jar but on what goes in the jar.

2. On strips of paper (use beads for children who aren't old enough to write, struggle with writing, or simply don't want to write), ask the child to write one thing they are good at and then put the strip of paper (or bead) into the jar.

3. Tell the child that it can be difficult to identify things we're good at (you can use a personal example to help normalize this for the child) and help them come up with ideas. Good ideas for children who cannot think of anything are "I'm good at waiting until I'm sure" or "I'm good at taking my time to decide." Virtually any negative can be turned into a positive.

4. As the child comes up with things they are good at, affirm each one, and have them place the strip of paper (or bead) into the jar.

5. Allow the child to take the jar with them, and give them extra beads or slips of paper so they can continue to add to their jar at home. Encourage the child to do this activity with parents, finding new things they are good at. As you continue working with the child, acknowledge their progress or ability to manage emotions by referring back to this technique and saying, "This is something else you're good at. Maybe you can add this to your jar."

TECHNIQUE FIFTEEN

BAG OF BAD
FEELINGS

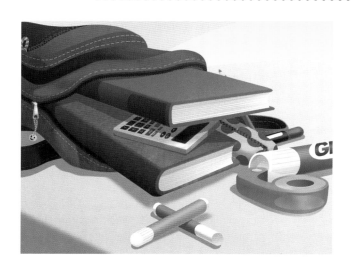

15 BAG OF BAD FEELINGS

MATERIALS NEEDED

blanket (or backpack), objects in your office

WHO CAN BENEFIT

Kids who are overwhelmed, take on too much, have trouble setting boundaries with friends, or who are perfectionists

WHY IT WORKS

This technique gives kids a tangible representation of what they are carrying emotionally. It gives kids an opportunity to feel the weight of emotional baggage and to feel the relief when they let go of something.

HOW TO IMPLEMENT:

1. Place either a blanket or a backpack in the center of the room or on a table.

2. Ask the child to go around your office and choose objects to represent all of their bad feelings at the moment—or what they are carrying emotionally. For example, a child might choose a thick book to represent their parents' divorce or a stapler to represent a friend problem. Ask the child to place the items in the blanket or backpack until all of their bad feelings are represented.

3. Then ask the child to wear the backpack or carry the blanket around your office for a few minutes, feeling the weight of the emotions or bad feelings. Talk about all the things in the backpack, how it feels to carry the weight, and how tiring it is to keep carrying it.

4. Once the child has done this for a few minutes, ask them, "What are you willing to let go of?" Allow the child to remove one piece of emotional baggage at a time, naming the bad feeling as they remove it. As the child takes each object out of the blanket or backpack, discuss how it feels to have less weight on their shoulders. Removing larger objects will make the bag noticeably lighter while removing smaller objects might not make much difference.

5. Encourage the child to practice this technique at home when feeling overwhelmed. This will help them see when they take on too much and have trouble letting go.

CONCLUSION

I hope you found many of these techniques useful. You might not use all of them, but I hope there are some you will use time and time again. These techniques were not created out of thoughts I had or ideas about what would help children. They were created while working with children who I struggled session after session to help.

When talking alone didn't work with these kids, I began to try different activities to connect with them and get them to share. Over time (and after countless trips to Dollar General), I developed a catalog of techniques that could access the inner lives of children in a way I couldn't have otherwise. The techniques are a starting point—a place to begin—as you build your own counseling program and develop your own style and way of working with children.

Other Books in the 15-Minute Series

15-Minute Focus is a new series that aims to help school counselors, administrators, and educators overcome three of the biggest challenges they face:

- **Limited Time** to manage the number of students for whom they are responsible
- **Mental Illness Stigma**
- and **Budget Constraints for Ongoing Training**

15MinuteFocusSeries.com

15-Minute Focus - Self-Harm and Self-Injury: When Emotional Pain Becomes Physical
Brief Counseling Techniques that Work
Leigh Bagwell

This book offers an in-depth look at the who, what, and why of self-harm; more accurately called nonsuicidal self-injury (NSSI). Discover types of NSSI behavior, the relationship between self-harm (NSSI) and suicidal ideation, signs and symptoms, protocols for schools to follow and how parents and schools can help. Includes reproducibles.

15-Minute Focus - Depression: Signs and Strategies for Educators, Students, and Families
Brief Counseling Techniques that Work
Melisa Marsh

This book provides a comprehensive look at depression and its effects on children and teenagers. Discover symptoms of depression, different types of depressive disorders, and how to identify depression versus sadness. Learn about the connection between depression and other mental illnesses, how school staff can support students with depression, and the successful management of depression. Includes reproducibles.

15-Minute Focus - Behavioral Threat Assessment and Management for K-12 Schools
Brief Counseling Techniques that Work
Melissa A. Louvar Reeves

This book explains the interrelated factors that play a role in a person's decision to plan and carry out an act of violence. Discover why and how schools should establish BTAM teams and protocols, identifying and reporting concerns, how teachers, administrators, counselors and the community can work together to mitigate troubling behavior and ensure student success. Includes reproducibles.

15-Minute Focus - Trauma and Adverse Childhood Experiences
Brief Counseling Techniques that Work
Melissa A. Louvar Reeves

This book gives counselors and educators a primer on how to support students who have experienced trauma. It covers different types of stress and symptoms, explanation of commonalities between externalizing disorders and trauma and stressor related disorders, and strategies for school mental health professionals, educators, administrators, and parents. Includes reproducibles.

15-Minute Focus - Suicide: Prevention, Intervention, and Postvention
Brief Counseling Techniques that Work
Melisa Marsh

This book gives school counselors and educators a step-by-step primer on how to navigate the death of a student or staff member by suicide. You will learn specific language to use when talking about suicide, strategies for implementing suicide prevention, suicide intervention, and suicide postvention programs, research and data to help communicate risk factors, and ways to support students in a virtual environment. Includes reproducibles.

15-Minute Focus - Grief: Processing and Recovery
Brief Counseling Techniques that Work
David A. Opalewski

This book offers school counselors and educators a primer on how to handle the death of a student or staff member. You will learn the concepts and implementation process of "comfort before counseling," grief research and data for children and adolescents, and grief support group setup. Includes reproducibles.

15-Minute Focus - Anxiety: Worry, Stress, and Fear
Brief Counseling Techniques that Work
Leigh Bagwell

This book gives counselors and educators a step-by-step primer on how to support students who struggle with anxiety. You will get an understanding of anxiety and clarification of anxiety vs. misbehavior, a breakdown of various anxiety disorders and how they present, and helpful tips for parents who have anxious children. Includes reproducibles.

Other books from Allison Edwards!

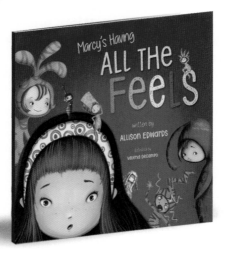

Marcy's Having All the Feels

Happy is all Marcy wanted to be. She didn't want to feel angry or jealous, and she didn't like feeling sad or embarrassed. One day, when Marcy's feelings disappear, she learns that her feelings don't have to control her and they might even have a function. And that one discovery? Well, it changes everything!

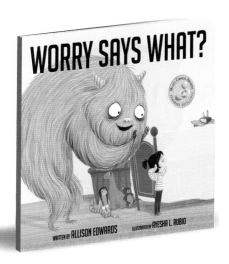

Worry Says What?

Worry and anxiety are currently the top mental health issues among children and teens. Children have a number of worries throughout childhood that will come and go. The problem is not with the worries themselves, but that children believe the worries to be true. With a relatable story and beautiful artwork, *Worry Says What?* will help children (and adults!) flip their thinking when anxious thoughts begin and turn them into powerful reminders of all they are capable of accomplishing.

Allison Edwards

COUNSELOR, AUTHOR, AND SPEAKER

Allison Edwards LPC, RPT is an affiliate professor in the Human Development Counseling department at Vanderbilt University. She is also the author of *Why Smart Kids Worry*, *Worry Says What?*, and *Marcy's Having All the Feels*, and the creator of "Anxiety Tracker," an iPhone app that helps track anxiety. Allison received her graduate degree in Counseling from Vanderbilt University and is a National Certified Counselor, Licensed Professional Counselor, and Registered Play Therapist. Allison has over 20 years experience working as a school teacher, school counselor, child/adolescent psychotherapist, and educational consultant to schools throughout the country

Allison travels both nationally and internationally training professionals in the areas of empowering anxious children in the classroom, managing the emotional needs of students, recognizing the social/emotional needs of gifted students, and sharing how educators can talk to parents about student anxiety. Allison helps school leaders understand how social/emotional differences can be supported in their neurologically diverse student populations, and provides consultation and staff development on how to effectively improve emotion regulation in the classroom.

Connect with Allison online at allisonjedwards.com